MW01154022

Mountain Gorillas

by Kaitlyn Duling

BELLWETHER MEDIA • MINNEAPOLIS, MN

BLASTOFF!
2
READERS

Blastoff! Readers are carefully developed by literacy experts to build reading stamina and move students toward fluency by combining standards-based content with developmentally appropriate text.

Level 1 provides the most support through repetition of high-frequency words, light text, predictable sentence patterns, and strong visual support.

Level 2 offers early readers a bit more challenge through varied sentences, increased text load, and text-supportive special features.

Level 3 advances early-fluent readers toward fluency through increased text load, less reliance on photos, advancing concepts, longer sentences, and more complex special features.

★ **Blastoff! Universe**

Reading Level

Grade K

Grades 1–3

Grade 4

This edition first published in 2021 by Bellwether Media, Inc.

No part of this publication may be reproduced in whole or in part without written permission of the publisher. For information regarding permission, write to Bellwether Media, Inc., Attention: Permissions Department, 6012 Blue Circle Drive, Minnetonka, MN 55343

Library of Congress Cataloging-in-Publication Data

Names: Duling, Kaitlyn, author.
Title: Mountain Gorillas / Kaitlyn Duling.
Description: Minneapolis, MN : Bellwether Media, 2021. | Series: Blastoff! readers : Animals of the mountains | Includes bibliographical references and index. | Audience: Ages 5-8 | Audience: Grades K-1 | Summary: "Relevant images match informative text in this introduction to mountain gorillas. Intended for students in kindergarten through third grade"-- Provided by publisher.
Identifiers: LCCN 2020041143 (print) | LCCN 2020041144 (ebook) | ISBN 9781644874141 (library binding) | ISBN 9781648340918 (ebook)
Subjects: LCSH: Mountain gorilla--Juvenile literature.
Classification: LCC QL737.P94 D85 2021 (print) | LCC QL737.P94 (ebook) | DDC 599.884--dc23
LC record available at https://lccn.loc.gov/2020041143
LC ebook record available at https://lccn.loc.gov/2020041144

Editor: Kieran Downs   Designer: Brittany McIntosh

Printed in the United States of America, North Mankato, MN.

Table of Contents

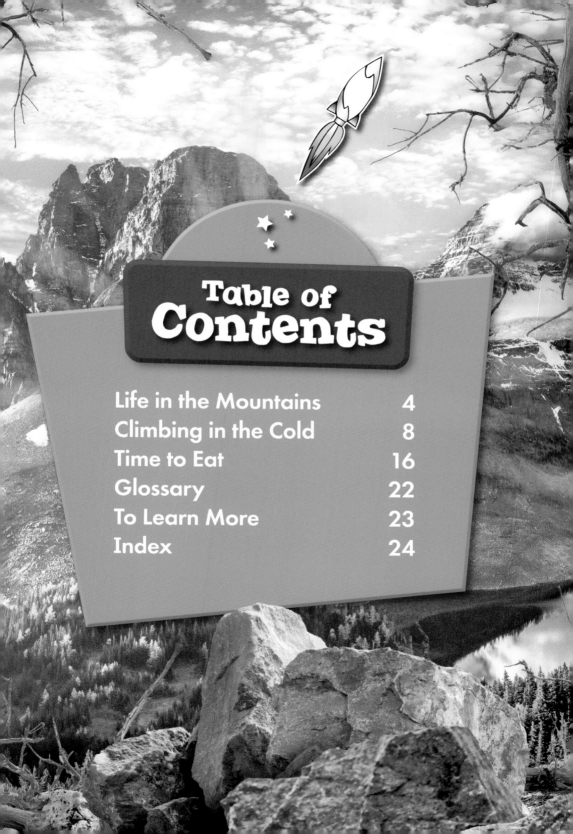

Mountain gorillas are large **primates**. They live in mountain forests in central Africa.

These gorillas are well **adapted** to their **biome**.

Mountain Gorilla Range

N
W E
S

range =

Mountain gorillas live at very high **elevations**. Their homes can be cold.

Long, thick fur keeps mountain gorillas warm.

Climbing in the Cold

Mountain gorillas travel a lot.
They walk on their hands
and feet.

Special Adaptations

long, thick fur

thick, padded skin

opposable thumbs

Thick, padded skin protects them from getting cut by rough rocks.

Mountain gorillas have **opposable** thumbs and toes. These help the gorillas build nests in trees.

Their hands and feet can **grip** branches. This makes climbing easier.

Mountain gorillas
live in groups.
They **communicate**
with each other.

They use faces, sounds,
and **gestures**.
The gorillas understand
each other.

Mountain Gorilla Stats

Least Concern	Near Threatened	Vulnerable	Endangered	Critically Endangered	Extinct in the Wild	Extinct

conservation status: endangered

life span: up to 50 years

13

On cold days, gorillas stay near their nests. They sit still for most of the day.

Groups gather together to stay warm.

Mountain gorillas are **herbivores**. They gather plants from the forest.

They eat leaves, tree bark, and flowers.

Mountain Gorilla Diet

giant lobelia

tree heather

African redwood bark

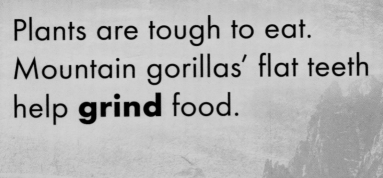

Plants are tough to eat. Mountain gorillas' flat teeth help **grind** food.

Special **bacteria** in their bodies also help break down food.

Mountain gorillas
rarely need to drink.
The plants they eat
give them enough
water to survive.

The mountains are
a happy home for
these gorillas!

Glossary

adapted—well suited due to changes over a long period of time

bacteria—single-celled living things that can only be seen with a microscope

biome—a large area with certain plants, animals, and weather

communicate—to share information and feelings using sounds, faces, and actions

elevations—the heights of places

gestures—movements of body parts, especially the hands and head

grind—to break or crush into small pieces

grip—to hold tightly

herbivores—animals that only eat plants

opposable—related to thumbs and toes that are able to move to touch the other fingers or toes of a hand or foot

primates—animals that use their hands to grasp food and other objects; primates are related to humans.

To Learn More

AT THE LIBRARY

Best, Arthur. *A Gorilla's Nest.* New York, N.Y.: Cavendish Square, 2019.

Furstinger, Nancy. *Animal Weightlifting Stars.* Mankato, Minn.: Child's World, 2017.

Huddleston, Emma. *Gorillas.* Minnetonka, Minn.: Kaleidoscope Pub., 2019.

ON THE WEB

FACTSURFER

Factsurfer.com gives you a safe, fun way to find more information.

1. Go to www.factsurfer.com.

2. Enter "mountain gorillas" into the search box and click 🔍.

3. Select your book cover to see a list of related content.

Index

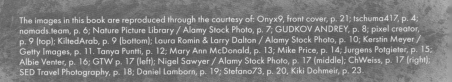

The images in this book are reproduced through the courtesy of: Onyx9, front cover, p. 21; tschuma417, p. 4; nomads.team, p. 6; Nature Picture Library / Alamy Stock Photo, p. 7; GUDKOV ANDREY, p. 8; pixel creator, p. 9 (top); KiltedArab, p. 9 (bottom); Laura Romin & Larry Dalton / Alamy Stock Photo, p. 10; Kerstin Meyer / Getty Images, p. 11. Tanya Puntti, p. 12; Mary Ann McDonald, p. 13; Mike Price, p. 14; Jurgens Potgieter, p. 15; Albie Venter, p. 16; GTW p. 17 (left); Nigel Sawyer / Alamy Stock Photo, p. 17 (middle); ChWeiss, p. 17 (right); SED Travel Photography, p. 18; Daniel Lamborn, p. 19; Stefano73, p. 20, Kiki Dohmeir, p. 23.